Power of

MW01297871

use the perfect words and phrases

to captivate women

By Fillmore Slim

Table of Contents

Introduction

You might be messing up with your chances to get a lovely lady to date, when you make calls that you do not know where to go next after the initial greeting and "how are you doing" part of the call. You should not burry yourself in bad experiences that you have gone through so far, because here is an eBook that will give you a different direction of introducing yourself to lovely women and striking a conversation that will lead to a productive date. The solution that this book provides is in the techniques of texting, because you do not have to reach to a lady through a call only.

Texting can do wonders when done in the right way, and that is what we are going to show you in this book. We know facing a lady for the first time is always very nervous and this is where many men fail, when they walk away feeling like losers and the ladies are left wondering what a coward you are.

Text messaging has become popular in the recent past and many people have switched from other means of communication to texting, because of the various advantages that it presents. These advantages are the level of privacy it provides, the simplicity in passing forth the message, the reduced cost of communications and the emotions you can show in the texting itself through the various add-ons texting applications are coming with, such as the emoticons.

The information in this book has been narrowed down to using texting as a tool to lure a lady and make her want to be with you and stick with you as your woman. When used properly, texting will reveal the kind of person you are and the lady will be able to know the kind of a man she is giving her time to. Eventually she will make her mind whether to agree to your request or simply throw your pleas to the usual dustbin of losers.

The battle starts when you plan to engage a certain lady in a conversation, because the process of asking her for the number is an action that gives many men Goosebumps. Not to worry, we will show you how to take that first step and get the vital number that will link you to that lovely lady who is giving you sleepless nights when you think of how lovely she is, and how much you want to spend time with her.

We however need to get some facts right before we get too much into the power of texting when you want a woman. Your failure to get the lady you want may be due to poor interaction or communication techniques, and the fact that you can type some lovely words on your Smartphone instead of voicing them does not guarantee that the lady will accept your requests. You need to do it right to get her attracted to you. The rejection you may have been facing could be as a result of your approach, and that is what you need to change when it comes to texting.

The texting style should create enough rapport and attraction for the lady you want to spend your precious time with, and the effort should not go down the drain because the connection of the hard work should be solid. Have a look at how you are supposed to initiate a conversation that will lead to great friendship.

Chapter 1: Getting Her Phone Number the right way

We must all admit that getting a girl's number is one of the most unnerving first steps when you want to start a relationship. Many of us have screwed up at this initial point of wanting to know a person, and this book will show you the right way to do it without being nervous or fearful of what you are doing. Remember those who fail in getting a lady's phone number are unsuccessful because they do it in the wrong way, because there is definitely the right way to ask for a girl's number that will lead you to success, and there is the wrong way, which will always make you look like a dunderhead and eventually you are rejected.

Let us first start by looking at the wrong way, so that we can correct the moves and enable you to be a winner when you set to go for your target's number.

The Wrong Way of Asking for the number – Avoid making it sound as if you are borrowing permission to have her number. Most men will always go like... "Can I get your number?" This to say the least makes you appear way much below the level of the woman you want to hoop up. You need to show value in your approach, and the style of asking for the number is one way to portray your value. Do not make it appear as if you are desperately in need of that number, but at the same time put it in a way that you seriously want to have a way of communicating with the girl.

It can be a tricky affair but it is doable anyway. You are not inferior in any way in this situation, and you should not let it look that way through asking for the number. When you ask the number in a way that sounds like asking for permission, the lady will take it as if you are not confidence. You will also show a sense of insecurity by being that low in asking for the phone number. Insecurity is a massive turnoff for all women. Do you want to turn the attractive woman off before you even reveal your feelings to her? The obvious answer is no, and so you should be bold enough when going for it.

You request should not elicit a "Yes" or "No" answer, because when you phrase your request like the example of the question above, the target will not have an option but to give you an affirmative or negative answer. This puts you in a bad situation because you have a 50% chance of getting a rejection.

Some men think that by offering their phone numbers first to the lady they need to get a number from will make the lady want to give them the number. If you do not have the lady's number, then offering yours first appears far far off the mark. What you are trying to tell her is that she should look for you by calling you later after the meeting and that is a bi NO for ladies. If you have gotten the number from the woman then you can request to offer yours back.

Feminism has been with us since time immemorial and their attitude never changes. There is no time a woman will go for a man and hence offering your number is the last thing that should cross your mind when you want to start initiate a connection. Socially, it is not acceptable for a woman to pursue man although there are exceptions, but you should never expect a woman to call you back first after the first meeting, when you leave your number instead of requesting for her number.

A beauty who appears to be pursuing men is perceived as a desperate woman who has failed to attract men naturally. No one wants to be branded a slut and lose face in the process of trying to get a man. Therefore, you will offer your number but be prepared to wait forever for that call.

The women will not also want to kill the fantasy that comes with being hunted for, and taking the number and acting on it means that she will not get the chance of enjoying that romantic feeling when you trying to lure her into your nest. They will always look forward to being seduced and if you are not in a position to do it, there is always another option for a woman.

That is the wrong way of asking for a number of a beauty that you want so badly, and next we show you how you should go about it.

The Right Way of asking for the Number – After understanding how you should not ask for a number from a woman, now you know that you should not makes is a request for permission to have it. A yes or no answer should not be the reply that request. The situation begs the question of how then should you request for the number if both of the mostly used ways are not the best ways to do it.

The way out of this situation is to be completely dominant by asking for the number directly. For example "I would like you to give me your number" or "Let us exchange numbers" by going for it this way, the lady will not have a big chance of refusing to offer the number, and you also put her in a corner that he does not have the flexibility of refusing what you are asking for.

Dominance elicits attraction in women and when you show it from the word go, the lady will have that attraction to you by seeing how determined you are to go for what you want. Even back in the days the most dominate males had the opportunity of amassing most of the resources that could offer food, clothing and shelter, and the rule of the jungle also dictates that survival is only for the fittest. Women are wired to sexually prefer the dominant men, who they can sire strong, dependable and dominating offspring just like their father.

Ladies hate stalkers just as men do, but we cannot deny that we do more of the stalking than them. For that reason, you should let a lady be aware that you will not be stalking her when you get the number, and that can be by preparing her before she offers the number. You can start by asking her if she has ever been stalked and how it went, then air your dislike for the act and affirm how you can never so that to a person.

Be smart when asking for that number and wrap your request in a statement that touches on your conversation. For instance, you can pretend that your time is up, obviously after enjoying the nice talk with this beauty that you have a great attraction to, and then tell her to give you her number so that you can continue the conversation on text. To let her know that you are not a stalker, you can joke a little bit by asking her to promise that she will not stalk you buy sending an avalanche of messages in a single day. I insist that the stalking part should be a joke that passes the message because if you make it look so serious she might misunderstand you and think you are taking her to be very desperate for you.

Asking for the number boldly does not justify that you will get it without a bit of sweating. You will be attracted to her but making her be attracted to you is not that easy. That is why you will get answers such as "I do not give my number to people that I do not know" or "It is not normal for me to give my number this fast." You have to make her feel attracted to you by telling her you would want to take the conversation further but time is not on your side. Be direct to and tell her you want to know her in depth or that you would want to be taken for a tour of the locality because you just moved in recently.

The bad news is that she may still object to your pleas. What do you next when you feel that you have done most of eliciting attraction from her side? Cool down, that should be your first reaction. Be a joker at times and tell her that you will be calling her just a number of times in a day, and if either of you becomes boring to the other, the calling can stop and you just maintain normal friendship. Still insist that evening nothing develops between the two of you, you will not be offended.

The objective is to make her feel less at risk when she gives you her phone number, and if your moves do not yield any fruits then you are not lucky with that beauty. However, when you do it right after having a mature and straight conversation, then you will get the number and we can now move on to the next level of the techniques you should use in texting the lady that you have lured to your nest.

Chapter 2: The techniques of texting a woman

A conversation that is based on purely texting gives you enough freedom to say all you want without the interruptions as experienced in calls or a face-to-face talk. You can send as many messages as you like but remember there is a way to do it, because you can mess you r relationship through the way you use your words. In this book, we are going to show you the techniques that you should use to make your texting a success, and you will never feel detached from your partner again, or a lady that you want to nest. Texting has power but that is only when you use it right, here are some of the techniques that you can apply.

Do not wait too long – After you secure the number you want from the lovely woman, do not keep her waiting for too long. She accepted to give you the number and hence she will be waiting for you to get back to her. If she had not been interested then you would not be having her number.

Remember that your first text to her is your everything regarding the direction that your togetherness will take. That text will help you succeed or if you do it the wrong way, it will be the end of the road for that relationship.

Keep them short and sweet – Avoid sending long texts as if you are trying to give her your history. The trick is to keep her engaged with short text of wanting to know how she is doing. It should make her feel special that you want to know how she is fairing. The text should also elicit response from her.

Let her miss you – Once you have gotten used t each other through texting. Suspend the process from your end and stop replying to the texts too. Take some time off for the day and only rekindle the texting the following day, without explaining your absence.

Here come the emoticons – It does not matter how funny you are in real life, but the reality is that you cannot show your playfulness through texting. The good news is that modern mobile platforms and applications are coming with sophisticated features such as emoticons, which you can insert in your texting to convey the feelings you have to the woman.

The blank message technique – I bet you have ever sent a blank message to a person but you did not intend to, and the person maybe replied with a call or a message, right? This can however work to your advantage but this time you will be doing it knowingly.

Make your texting lively and lovely even when you are coming to an end of the conversation, where the woman will give you a goodnight kiss expecting you to offer one back, and you do. Do not stop there, wait for a few seconds and send a blank text and she will definitely respond, where your response will be that she is faking it and that she wants another kiss while she has given only one. Such teases will keep the woman want to initiate a texting session the next day and there you will have a budding relationship.

Where a woman is teasing you with some texts that you do not have material to reply to, you can use the blank texts and call it a special silent treatment once she protests about it. You can even say that you are knocking on her to find out if she is still there, and then be open that you are simply tricking her.

Perfect timing – Delaying replies is a huge turnoff to both women and men. Do not make your newly found beauty keep n waiting for your replies for too long because she will obviously think that you are busy with something else at your end, and she is just an add on to your activities. Still on the same, you should control the speed of your replies because if you reply by sending multiple messages within a short time, they will end up offending her.

You can try more texting techniques that will lead you to winning the heart of the woman you just met, and the secret is to use them wisely and align them to the liking of the person you are targeting, and you will succeed effortlessly.

Chapter 3: When and How to Send the First Text

Most people will feel uneasy when they think of texting a lady that they have just gotten her number. It is a usual feeling and hence one should not be too worried about it, but what many men wonder is when to send that first text. It depends on the time that you have acquired the number from her. Morning hours people are busy and hence they do not have the time to chat to a point of exchanging number and therefore you will mostly find that you will have the number in the evening.

Even when you get the number at daytime, texting the woman does not feel so right because most people are busy during the day. The impact of your first text will not be felt as expected when the text finds the targeted person busy. In that case, waiting for the evening hours just after dinnertime would be the best timing for the first text. This ensures that the lady does not have many distractions and hence will give your text the attention it requires, and be sure to have composed it perfectly to initiate a conversation.

Do not wait for the next morning to send that first text, do it the same night after your first meeting. The reason is because the woman will also be waiting for your first move and if you keep her waiting for too long, you might spoil the excitement and when you do it later on, after two days maybe, the impact will be too light to yield good results.

The Content of that first text

Now that we understand that the lovely lady should not be kept waiting for your first text, next is what the text should contain, because many men mess it up here by starting or the wrong footing hence sending the wrong signals to the new catch. You may have the very best of the intentions but your first text ruins it. The following are some of the ways you should initiate a conversation.

Do it jokingly – You can start with something like "wait a minute, have you seen where I have put my wallet?" Be sure to start with her name to avoid confusion on her side. At that time of the day in a house that she has never been to, the joke will crack her with laughter. From there you can then continue it by saying that you have watched something on the TV that reminds you of the conversation you had previously. You can then request whether you can carry on with the conversation on text.

You definitely want to continue seeing the lovely lady you met and there is no better way to make the request than via text. You can tell her that you enjoyed every moment that you had at day time, and the come up with a day that you would want to meet her again. Ask her if she will be available on that particular day.

After that, you will need to stop being too taut in your approach and you can change and be a bit flirty. An example of how you should do that is "It is too bad that we just parted abruptly, I wish we had a chance to make out." Before she even gets a chance to answer that, you can wrap it with another question such as "By the way I forgot to ask, and this is vital to me; do you like going to movie theatres?" From there you can enquire the kind of pass time she enjoys and then you can align yourself to her liking so that you can have some great time together.

As long as you get the opener right and the lady accepts tow the line, you will be set for a lovely text interaction that will lead to a thriving relationship as long as you both play it safe. Do not be too excited about the progress you make with your initial part of befriending the woman, there are a number of things that may derail your progress and that is what we will look at next.

Chapter 4: Things that may affect the progress of your conversation

The conversation you initiate should be kept alive to ensure that the woman feel your presence every time her mind gets off her busy schedule. It should not be like stalking though, but you should do it in a manner that you stay relevant in her mind, and she will always be expecting to hear from you. Below are tips on how you should maintain a constant progress of the togetherness.

Waiting too long before keeping the conversation going – Some people think that holding back for some time when you are supposed to be communicating with a new found love is a fancy thing, but the reality is that you will only end up frustrating the lady by making her think that you got fed up with the communication.

When you have gotten into a smooth conversation with your newly found woman, she will want to keep it going because a new relationship becomes very exciting to women. They want to take it to the highest level possible, and so when you stop communicating she may get demoralized and you will lose her as soon as you got her.

Right Reaction for delayed replies – Girls will play mean too at times by delaying replies, just to make you feel the urge to get to them. Reaching out to them because of the delayed replies gives them a rush of adrenaline because it is one way to make them feel appreciated, loved and special. However, you should not misinterpret the tactic and think that she was fed up with you and maybe you are boring her.

Relax and give it time, and avoid all the negative reasons that you may be thinking about. Her ex has not come back yet, she is not losing interest in you and it is not that she is not ready to let you into her life. Keep off these negative thoughts and let nature take its course. Thinking about the delayed replies will only pile stress on you for nothing.

Some girls play it tough and decide not to respond to your texts or even cancel plans that you had agreed on, for instance going for dinner. When this happens, keep your cool and ignore that you felt bad about it, although deep inside we know you will be hurting as hell, and wait for the time she will respond.

The waiting should not be too long though, give her a couple of days before you reach out to her again. If she was just playing it rough, she will come up and give a small apology and an excuse too. At times, they do not want to appear as if they are running to you. However, the lady might behave the same again and being a man, you have to show your worth and let it go. Do not reach out to her because if she is interested she will get back to you.

The point is not to give up when you experience such a reaction from a newly found beauty. Give it a bit of time until she settles down and believes that you seriously want her.

Wondering why she is acting ignorant – Making a woman feel attracted to you is not a walk in the park. You need to understand that it requires a lot of patience, hard work, perseverance and humbleness. The feelings of a woman are very fragile and hence you will need to take her as she is, given that you are both strangers to each other, and she needs time to learn you and either accept or reject your approach.

Having said that, you need to know that people are different and while some will be quick to give in, others will take days to dance to your tune. The good thing about being at a level where you are communicating is that most women will not want to hurt your feelings through rejecting you. They hate dramas that come up through confrontations because they eventually end up ugly.

There nature of wanting to be good throughout makes them step back and allow nature to take its course, where you can get to a point of giving up or pushing for more attention. If you react negatively, the lady will justify her instincts and assume you were not her type, but when you show more interest and continue the push positively you will end up winning her heart.

A girl may not be into you at first but according to the way they are wired she cannot bring herself to tell you off or they do not have any feelings for you. That is why you will note the ignorant nature in them. It does not last if at all you can understand that she was not just there waiting for you as her ultimate man, you need to plant that seed of being attracted you so that she can give you the attention you want, and reply your texts promptly.

Good things do not come easily and so you have to work hard to get the beautiful woman you met. You will definitely get a "No" along the way and a number of them for that matter and you should not be hurt or dejected because of the initial rejection. Serious women will always do that to ensure that you seriously want to stick with them and not joking around.

Lashing out at a girl because she has rejected you for some time is not the solution to the situation. Many men do great things and even buy expensive gifts just to get acceptance, and eventually come out empty handed. Your effort however should be measured to know the resistance because you will definitely tell genuine resistance and when you have a chance to get a breakthrough.

Allow a girl to tell you the feelings that she has for you and ascertain that they are genuine. Telling you that she does not feel you is not the end of your effort because you can come up with a solution to what s making her not feel you. Try to get more information from her as much as you can but do not be too pushy because she may block you or ignore all the texts that come from you.

Only text her when she is willing to reply and when she goes dull you can back off a little bit, or even ask her when you can text her to find out a solution for the stalemate.

Keep your texting very cool and controlled because there is n woman who will take "yelling" messages kindly, and that may even be the end of your conversation. Go into the process of pursuing a woman with the understanding that there are two sides to a coin. You can be rejected or be accepted, but both processes take time. Ladies give initial conversation time to learn their suitors and the outcome of their assessment is what will make her reject your moves or give you thumbs up, and there you will have conquered another level in the approach to securing a space in the beautiful lady's heart.

Why the numbers you get do not yield – Have you ever wondered why every number you request from the ladies you meet never end up to a concrete relationship? Cool down because you are not an isolated case, because this happens to many other men around the world. We have a solution in this book, and the good thing is that you do not have to any further that inside your ability to get a solution to this. It all goes down to how you use the number that you have been given, because when a woman accepts to give you her number she leaves the ball in your court, and your experience and the will to go for the lady will make you win her.

In this situation, the girl's mandate is only to provide you with her number and you are supposed to do all that pertains to relationships to reach out to the beauty. In other words, you will have to initiate the interaction and move it forward. When it goes stale, simply understand that you did not do your best, and if you seriously want the woman, you have to push more for it. There is always hope if the woman has not put you off officially, because when a woman is seriously not interested in your move she will try all she can to tell you off. It may not be a blunt stop but every time you will be trying to reach out to her, she will keep on telling you that you are on the wrong path and you should try some place else.

Let us go back to your issues of having problems with making the purpose of acquiring a number happen. We stated previously that the main purpose of texting a woman that you have met and liked is to make her be attracted to you and organize for a date, where you will pour your heart out to her and make her know that it is always skipping a bit whenever you think of her. You will achieve that based on how you compose your texts, and the initial ones should be lovely, should and captivating. Texts that will make her want to re-read them every time when she is alone.

Start with fun texts that touch slightly on your attraction towards her, and the general things that brought you to her. The good thing about the initial texts is that you will be guided by her response, and that guide is what gives you material for the next replies. As the texting progresses, take the next step of "Hey, by the way we can have some drinks this coming Saturday, can you make some time for that?" Such requests however should be made after reading her previous replies that show she is already relaxed and can accept your company.

Most of the men are very afraid to put forth that question of whether she can be available for the date, but the fear is uncalled for because most ladies are always lying in wait for such moves, because she can never initiate the move. You may experience a bit of resistance, but that kind of resistance is the one that comes with a solution, or does not have that much weight to make your request fail to materialize. For instance, she can tell you... "I may not be available because am doing laundry in the morning hours." There she gives you the clue that she could have come were it not for the laundry that she will be doing in the morning, but then you will push her insisting that you will also be available in the evening, which is actually the right time to grab some coffee after the day. She will accept halfheartedly but deep inside she knows that she needs to meet with you.

Invite her to a dinner or a cup of coffee at some nice social location, where you can relax and engage in a deeper talk one-on-one. The time of inviting her to your home is not yet and hence avoid texting anything about having some good time at your place. The talk about your place should be long after you have been used to each other, or else when she asks questions about where you live. They always ask that in the initial stages of texting and knowing each other.

Rejections are natural and when she rejects your first invitation for a date, do not stop texting her. It might make her feel as if she wronged you, or maybe all you want is to get her as soon as you can. However, when you mean to ask her out for the date you should not dance around the issue. It will make her perceive you as a coward who does not know what he wants exactly. Text her and make it clear about your wish of having dinner, coffee or lunch at her own convenience. At this stage, everything should be based on the convenience of the girl, she is special and you want her to be happy with you, there is no way you can impose your convenience on her.

When you ask about the date openly, you have the opportunity to know if she is really interested in you, and so you will move on instead of spending your time obsessing about a person who does not even think about you.

On the other hand, when she accepts your invite you should not kill the conversion. Texting her periodically tells her that you are still thinking about her, and that the deal is still on. Periodic texting shows that the interest you had when you started sending her the messages, or when you talked her into giving you her number is still alive. Texting her to the point of setting a date is a great achievement. You should therefore protect that achievement by texting some greetings in the morning hours, or if you miss that you can enquired how her day was in the evening.

The point is to keep her alert that the date is still on your mind. We even make things up where you can tell her how you passed b the coffee house you intend to take her and enjoyed a cup of the drink, remind her that you know it could have been even better if she was present.

Confirmation of the date is done by texting her the day before the D-day. You want to know if the deal is still on and since it is not polite to ask her so directly, texting her the day before you will get a perfect answer of her position about it. The morning of the great day is a good time to check how the things are by texting and letting her know how excited you are, and h you wish the hours can rush by so that you meet her soon.

Her response to your texts will tell you if both of you are on the same page, or she opted to change the plans. It can be very heartbreaking t find out at the last minute that the date is not happening. Confirming it before you step out to go and get her will cushion your ego and feelings, and although you will be hurt and bit broken, the impact will not be as huge as when you get the news at the last minute.

Minimize your texting after you set the date of meeting. However, if the messages are coming from her end you should not ignore them. Reply to her texts as usual. You are the person in need of her company and hence the texting should not be ignored at all. In reality, you are the one who is supposed to slow it down, first to ensure that you do not kill the exciting tension, and secondly to save some of the serious and interesting topics that you need when you finally meet.

You need to have enough arsenals of topics and material to use at the day of the date. You do not want to sit there staring at each other, or only answering to her conversation's short questions.

Making the texting interesting as it progresses

Texting a girl can be a short-term or a long-term affair, depending on how you will handle it. There are men who cannot keep a girl engaged on text without losing it by lacking good things to tell the newly found friend, and eventually they both get bored to continue with the conversation. In these modern days where everything about communication is done through texting on different platforms such as Whatsapp, Facebook messaging, Imo, Viber and many more, one has to gather a lot of information on different topics to keep a conversation alive.

One way to do it is to find out the interest of the new love that you have found, so that you can base your conversations on the different interests. You can also try to introduce the things you like to her so that at some point, you can talk about them, and eventually she will accept them and play along.

However, you need to understand that when you keep the texting time too long and at regular intervals, you will be the one to lose. In reality, when you spend too much time on texting the newfound beauty, you lower the chance of meeting her in person because you will end up talking about the many things that can make you want to meet her.

You definitely want something to happen but achieving that can be very hard, if you do not have a way of making the girl miss to see you. The only way to make the woman miss you is to talk less but keep her engaged to know that you are always thinking of her. In addition to that, you should also understand that the effect of a physical talk cannot be compared to that of the conversation you have when texting. Facial expressions and gestures have special powers to make the girl feel loved, and they will always want you to keep talking to them even with your eyes.

The purpose of the special words you use while texting is to draw the girl towards you, and that is what you should work on so hard to make her respond positively to your invitation for the date.

Keep it interesting but do not overdo it because it might lose quality. The happy couples you see around did not get each other purely from texting each other, but the power of the initial part of their engagement was achieved through texting so that they can get used to each other.

Chapter 5: Having the right mindset in handling demotivating reactions

The texting guidance in this book is meant to equip you with the right tools to approach a woman and make her yours. You should be very careful with the wording of your texts because ladies are very sensitive with what you tell them. They can misinterpret pieces of information and turn them around to attack you, if you do not clarify what you say. Some comments or the way you start to text her can also have a different impact than what you intended, for instant starting with... "Hey girl, it's Steve" can sound bad to any girl because it does not have an element of courtesy in it. The statement is as if you are trying to alert her that you are available, and hence she can get ready to initiate a texting session, or be the one to ask you how you have been or what you are up to.

In the alternative setting, your texting should be something similar to... "Hey Nish, it was great to be with you, I enjoyed the coffee more so the talk we had. Have a perfect night and hope to talk to you soon —Joe."

That message should be after 24 hours. Ensure that you send a follow up message after a dinner date after an hour or so, before she forgets the fun you had that evening. You will be surprised at how the conversation will extend deep into the night, and by then you can make your expectations known by telling her why you liked and how happy you would like the happiness to continue.

At times, you may doubt the feelings of the lady that you have just met, and a short personal text will do the trick to find out if she was okay with the time you had. Highlight some instances that you noticed while you were having dinner like absentmindedness or a call that was not so clear, but make it appear like a joke because she might take it too seriously and conclude that you are taking her to be bad mannered.

It is very important to highlight every happening between you, for instance when she texts something that you do not find to be in line with a healthy relationship. Sometimes it turns out to be a mistake or a slip of the tongue, but if you just keep silent and make your own decisions, it might turn nasty afterwards. Question it in a polite way and you will find how cool your interaction will be. If it was not a mistake then you can explain why you found it to be weird or not right, and in saying so you clarify to him that she can ask you anything that she finds questionable. Being open with each other is how healthy relationships bud.

Handling the negative reactions

In most cases when you are starting a relationship, the lady will have a tendency of going against your wishes just to test how willing you are to have her by your side, and so you need to be very alert about it. She will cancel dates and give you reasons that do not justify her failing to come. The way you will handle the cancelation will determine her judgment. Always be positive in handling the situation and do not show any hurt about it.

For instance she may say that she will not be able to show up for the date because she is to help her friend with some chores, and given that you had planned for the whole week to hook up for the date, and is paramount that you will get a little bit disappointed. The reaction should not be that you were looking forward to seeing her and have some great time, claiming that you had no other plans for that evening apart from being with her, but you should hide your feelings and show some positivity about it.

On the contrary, tell her that you wish her a great time with the friend, and show some concern by telling her to take care. However, do not forget to tell her that you will want to steal her on the following Friday since you miss her a lot.

Girls are very sensitive about a man who will want to be too possessive. Since your communication is text based, find some comforting words when something negative comes up although you clearly know that she is trying to gauge your reaction when she objects to your requests. Text her in a way that will show her you care about her decision, and the things that will make her happy. After she is done with her activities, she can come back to you wholly.

If you really want her to come at the previously arranged time, still do not try to ask it in a way that suggests that you are idle and you were only waiting for her to have some good time. That will not make her change what she has decided to do and come to keep you company. It actually reveals that you do not have alternatives of filling your time and being active according to changes, let her be and be positive in your response. You can then try to playfully ask her to reschedule, but that should be a way of flirting with her, not that you really want her to change her plans.

Dealing with consistent cancelations – Some ladies are tough in handling their initial parts of a relationships and when you text her about a date that she confirms to show up, do not be excited because she will then cancel it in the last minute. The excuses she texts back are heartbreaking because for instance she can claim to be waking up early the next morning, and coming for the date may mess up her plans.

In reality, she could have given you a heads up about waking up early but you do not have to rub it in. Be positive again because the game of attracting a beauty depends on a high level of patience, perseverance and self-control. When she persists in canceling the plans that you have been making, then make it her responsibility to make it happen.

In this case, you should tell her that it is okay for her to take all the time that she needs and she should have a great time. The truth is that you still want to meet up with her maybe for the first date and experience the goodness that you see in her. For that case, your text should keep the deal open maybe by telling her to let you know when she is free so that you can grab some drinks and talk a bit. Wish her a good night and lovely time in the next coming busy day.

Sometimes we men text too much thinking that it will make the girl see how much you need her. That is not the case because some ladies, especially the ones who are professionals in playing hard to get games, will give you some hard time and if you are softhearted you will give up easily.

It is true that you want the cute girls very much, but let your texts not show that you are desperate for her. Remember texting is not the same as calling, if she is seeking for advice from her friends, the texts you send will be perfect material for them to counter your approach and give her the power to play hard to get. So, do not make it hard for yourself by chasing her with texts that show you are thinking of her too much or you can be available when she wants.

Being upset or aggressive when she cancels a dates for a number of times will be taken as immature and it is an attitude that turns girls off very easily. Avoid composing your text messages in a way to guilt-trip a girl in a bid to make her come and meet you. She has canceled the date a number of times and so you should respect your ego, stop following her too much and that will tell her that you too have standards. By so doing you will place the ball in her court and play the waiting game for her to initiate the texting again, and then you can play it by your rules.

Breaking the silence – We all know that as men, when we do not talk to a girl that we want for so long it hurts us inside and there is this strong urge to break the ice and listen to that sweet voice, or see her texting back. When you use the tactic above, that of keeping quiet and letting her come for you, it will get to appoint that you will have to text her and rekindle the conversation.

Girls can hold it back for very long because that is how they are wired. They know you are the one who is supposed to initiate a conversation, and so when you kill it you have to revive it yourself. Many a times are the ones that the man will have to come back and check on how the girl is doing, and do not be shocked that it will happen to you too.

Do not feel shamed because of that and do it professionally too. Some people reinitiate the conversation in a way that indicates that they do not remember whom they are texting. For instance, one may ask - "Hey, is this still June's phone number?" - And that can hurt the lady a great deal. The reason is that it will make him feel that she has already been forgotten and you are taking her as a stranger. She will think that you are trying to check the owner of the forgotten strange number in your phonebook.

An example of the right way to do it should be... "Hey, just seen a polka dot dress on the display that reminds me of your lovely short dress that hugs your body to shape, you still have it?"...the question is specifically meant elicit and answer that will lead to a short conversation and you will be good to go after that.

When rekindling a conversation, do it in a way that reminds the girl of the beautiful things that you did together if you had ever met, or the lovely things that highlight your first meeting. She might have found another guy when you were away, and you will now be facing a stiffer competition than you had before. In that case, start it on the right footing that makes her want to respond to your complement, a complement that is wrapped in some kind of a greeting and one that definitely requires response.

The next step should be to be true to yourself about the reason you thought of texting her, because she will definitely ask you how comes you have remembered her, and why you have been that silent. Do not hide your feelings, text her that you have been thinking of her and when it came to checking on her something such as a job activity could come in, but you finally could not hold it any more. Honesty wins the hearts of most ladies and when she realizes you are being truthful, you will automatically be in her good books again!

Lastly, when a girl acts busy and is seems like she will never make time for the date, be good and let her understand that you value her work the same as you do yours, and do not phrase it like you are feeling bad about her being busy.

Show her how cool it is to be busy and because of her diligence, it will be very easy to complete the tasks. Turn every challenge that she brings on to be an opportunity to pull her towards you. When you show her how easy it is to work on her assignment, ask her how she would like to celebrate her triumph. That is when you throw the final dice and ask her out for dinner or a cup of coffee, and gauging with her response throughout the texting you will tell if it will be a winning situation, which it definitely is.

Chapter 6: Handling anxiety if you are not used texting a woman

Anxiety is a main factor that leads to failure when it comes to befriending a woman through texting. One can never tell what is happening on the mind of a woman on the other end, when the reply to a text takes longer than usual. However, patience is the only trick that can be used to conquer the effects of anxiety, because when you react you might mess a situation that was okay all along. For example, when she does not reply within the expected time, you might think that she is ignoring you and if you rush to ask her that while she delayed because she was a bit busy you may mess the whole situation.

What a man needs to agree first before he even starts texting a lovely lady is that texting itself is very stressing, when you are using it to win the heart of a woman. There is no much difference between face-to-face conversations and texting as it was some years back, because you can show any feelings you want to the person you are texting, and the emoticons used are creating images on the minds of the participants, which make it feel like the person is next to you.

It therefore becomes very unnerving to engage a girl in a deep conversation about wanting her, but you have no other option but to go for it through texting. It actually feels just like it did when you tried to talk your first girl into liking your, only that this time it is a bit tense due to the seriousness at which you want the lovely lady.

Some people believe that texting a woman is tougher than speaking to her face to face. In-person gestures make conversation simpler and you can even tell the progress of your effort by looking at her facial expressions or even body language.

In texting, you are only left to imagine her instant reaction to your messages, and woe unto you if he takes longer than expected to reply to those texts.

Another thing is that you cannot use sarcasm and vulgarity to your advantage like you can do in a verbal conversation. Try that on text and it will come out badly you will wish you never tried it. Those styles of texting can only apply to a person who you have been used to, and who understands your sarcastic or vulgar nature. To a newfound girlfriend it will be a suicidal move regarding the friendship, and it may even end there.

There is the main anxiety that engulfs a person when he thinks of starting to engage a person in a text conversation, but there is the other major situation of the anxiety that is experienced between text messages. I bet you always feel the strong urge to know what is coming when you see that 'typing...' indicator when your partner is replying to your texts. When the topic is hot, sometimes the situation becomes unbearable and you may even walk around the room in readiness for responses.

The 'typing...' already indicates to you that something is on the way and there is nothing you can do to change the forthcoming message. Depending on what you had written the level of anxiety can be enormous.

When trying to reach out to your girlfriend and you are embroiled in an argument, you will definitely say things in the heat of the exchange and the tree dots that show up after your tough reply tells you that the bomb is about to explode. You do not know what is coming and this is a major source of the anxiety.

When having a text exchange life can be a bit easier but when it gets to a situation where she does not text you back, it can be really hard on you. Imagine sending a text in the evening and the reply does not come until the next day, where you will not even get an apology but the continuation of the conversation. If you get yourself in such a situation, do not overreact or start thinking about negative things. Just give it time because she might be giving it time to see what kind of a man you are. Do not let anxiety get the best of you and mess a situation that could have been natured.

To deal with anxious situations you should first learn the king of a girl you are dealing with, so that you can understand her daily activities, what she does when she gets to the house in the evening, whom she stays with, her social status and many other things that defines her life. When you understand her that way, you will be in a position to text her at the right time you will definitely get a timely reply that will reduce the time of waiting by a bigger margin.

Be lively in your style of texting and ensure that what you send her is interesting and evokes an instant reply. If she seems to be too slow in replying, reduce your intensity of texting her to match her replying speed. Looking for a better time that you should be texting her is another great idea of taming the anxiety. When a girl has ample time to read your texts, she will have the time to reply them too. Most texts that lack response are never read.

You learn a girl's style of texting from the first time you start texting. If anything changes from the usual style you know, then you can start to get anxious. For instance, if she starts replying your texts in monosyllables and she used to be detailed from the beginning, there might be something amiss about your engagement and you should investigate about it. Backtrack your engagement to the point where things stated being dull and you will find out the cause of the sudden change. Rectify the mishap and you will be back on the right track of communicating with your lovely lady without any difficulty.

Chapter 7: Texting that leads to the first date

Texting should not only be about exchanging messages but also should lead to an ultimate goal, and that goal is mainly a way to meet and have a one-on-one talk, know each other better and plan more meetings that will lead to a strong relationship that lasts.

You are the one to make the rules in this because she is the guest. That means that you have to come up with a probable date at time, and then ask her whether she is okay about it. The conversation that follows will be an organized way of finding the right day and time to fix the date.

There are times when you need the company of the lady badly that you cannot resist inviting her out. I say invite because that the way it should be. If you make it a question, remember that you have a 50% probability of not having her at your dinner table because she might answer negatively.

In that case, you can start by asking her what she is doing at that particular time, hoping that it is daytime, and then tell her that you need to take her out for dinner if she does not mind. That is after you find out that she will not be having a busy day and evening. Impromptu dates are fun and in most cases, they end p to be the start of a lovely relationship together.

When your friends have invited you to a party, you should not leave her behind. Girls become very secure when they are taken out to a party where your friends are, because they feel that you have nothing to hide and you can reveal your intentions of having her in your life even to your friends. Be social while out there and joke around with friends freely as you introduce her to everyone.

After the outing is over and everyone is back into the house, you can follow-up the reaction through texting to find out the impact of the date. Remember that in most cases girls tend to be open to you if they do not have eye contact when communicating, and the text follow up will be a good way to read and feel the progress of your effort.

Chapter 8: Texting the Girl after the first Date

The date has been lovely, you are back to your house, and you kick off your shoes to relax in the satisfaction of your achievement. Do not forget that the date was just the beginning of a long journey, and the texting does not end there.

The initial texts before you even knew each other well were tensing and the next ones after the date have their fair share of anxiety. It is not a walk in the park and you ought to be ready for some stressful moments when you embark on texting the lovely lady after the date. It even becomes tougher if you have a strong liking for the person.

The main purpose of this first text after the lovely time out should be to express gratitude to your partner, and you should compose it in a way t suggest that you need another date at her convenience. Do not be too praising but highlight the good things that you noted about her, and

63

tell her that you like it all because she just the character you expected. In this text, you have to be very true to yourself because the things you highlight about her are real and should show that you were keen on her behavior.

First dates are awesome and you may think that because you enjoyed yourself to the full the testing will be the simplest. No, you may have enjoyed everything but when it comes to putting it down on text, it can be very scary. Your date may have said that she had a great time when you parted, but you cannot tell the true feeling she has about that session. She may be as tense as you, not knowing where to start in appreciation. In that case, be the first one to open that door for conversation by sending a friendly text.

The trick here is to find a balance of the right time to start the texting. Starting too soon will make you be the clingy guy who does not want to give the girl a space to relax and thing about the escapade. You may even send her a text that is not cool and in the process mess the good ending to the outing. The girl needs some time to cool down and relax. You start texting immediately after you part and the girl will wonder what kind of a guy you will be when you both finally hook up and start dating seriously.

On the other hand, you still have to play by the rules of the very first texting where you should not stay for too long before you text her. When she gets back to her house, she already expects that you will knock on her and so you should not keep her waiting for that text for long. Send your post-date text within 24 hours. If it was a lunch date, then you should send it in the evening because she will obviously be busy during the day and you do not want to mess up with her work.

She will be more relaxed in the evening, which is a great time for her to read and let the message sink in. she will have the time to reply to your text too. The only text that you send some few minutes after you part should be that of checking whether she has arrived to her place safely. It is a good way of showing that you care about her and then you can wish her a good relaxation time, and do not forget to tell her that you will talk later after she has settled.

Saying thank you and being polite in the way you pass your gratitude message matters a lot, because there are obviously many things that you will have to thank your date for. Girls are special in the way they behave and act whenever they go, and you will see the truth about it when you start ordering in the restaurant you go to. They are always available to ensure that you order the right dessert and the things you will need in your time out.

Those are the small things that you should show gratefulness for, because it will make her feel very special when you not her simple effort. You may have called her for the date but it is very polite to call her and thank her for accepting to be with you, and gracing the outing.

Throughout the conversation, you should be very alert of the terminologies that you are using because some may reflect a different attitude and meaning, and you do not want to be seen as if you are pushing things too far. For instance using the word date in your texting removes the casualness of your outing and makes it seem as if you are concluding that the girl is already into you.

You do not have to be aggressive in drawing the girl to you and hence you should use simple terms that ensures the progress is smooth and natural. With every text just as you started courting the woman, make them lively and fun so that you can both enjoy the exchanges. Texting is fun and if you are not feeling the fun when exchanging texts with the lovely lady, then you may not have found the right girl yet, you may as well move on to get another suitor.

Chapter 9: Follow the rules of texting a woman

The rules of texting a woman ensures that you do not become too boring in your conversation, you can keep the conversation alive for long and in the whole process keep the girl attracted to your texting such that she will be looking forward to reading the texts you send her every time.

The rules we highlight here are simple but many men ignore putting them to practice and in the end, they mess up their engagements. You do not to be one of them and hence we outline them for your advantage. When you learn the following rules and stick to using them in your communications, you will be amazed at how lovely and enjoyable texting a woman will be.

Reciprocity Rule – Ignore using this rule at your own peril, and do not blame anyone when you are caught in the trap of neediness, and this trap is a top killer of attraction when it comes to relationships. The worst of it is when it comes from a man who keeps on sending their targeted women many messages without giving them the chance to reciprocate.

The way apply the rule of reciprocity is to monitor the amount of messages you send her per day and her replies. If the two do not balance, then you need to find a way to balance them either by reducing your amount or encouraging her to be replying to all your messages so that they can balance. Remember you cannot tell her openly that you need her to be sending more messages. Put it in a way that she will feel appreciated and want to do more of what is making get the appreciation, and hence she will increase the rate of replying to your texts involuntarily. For instance, you can tell her that you love receiving texts from her, and enquire if she can be sending them more often.

Forget after sending – Mostly men send texts and keep on staring on their phone screens waiting for the reply to pop up. It becomes excruciating when you have to wait for the next two hours just to get a three worded reply, or an excuse about the phone being on silent mode, I had misplaced it and such-like excuses.

The phone may be genuinely broken and hence waiting for a message to come will be a waste of your time, and revealing how needy you are. This rule is not to be applied on the rouge girls who are not interested in you, but it is for that special girl you want to maintain contact with for long.

Text to our loved ones must not have replies and that is why we can write them and forget about them, knowing the message will be passed and an answer will come at its right time. Such a text should not be composed in a way to elicit an answer or reply, and hence you should not write it in a form of a question. Let your text be informative so that you can send and forget about it.

Maintain good coordination – Only reply after she has sent you a text. It is just a means of communication but not a match where you have to hit back immediately after she sends or replies to your text. Send the text, wait for the reply and then reply accordingly, and the conversation will go on very smoothly.

Diversify your texting – Monotonous texting bores everyone and you can attest to that too. So, why send your lovely lady the same kind of texts every time? Love texts will get to a point where they will mean nothing, and so you have to change topics to make the conversation lively.

Change the time of sending too and you will see the improvement in your communication. When you get used to sending her messages at the same time of the day for example when she is going to sleep or in the morning, and the topic is still the same, it will get to a point where she will not be reading your texts, because she already knows what to expect.

Be a Teaser – Including some teasing in your texts makes them different and enjoyable to read, but you should do it spontaneously. You can tell her something like... "You are so cute my love...sometimes". Such comments cannot be said on daily basis because they might be misinterpreted and can cause a text fight easily.

Avoid text fights – When it comes to texting a topic that it is too tense, the best thing is to avoid it and you agree to carry on with it on call or when you meet each other. When you text bitter words they are usually misunderstood and the topic may escalate to a situation that will be tough to control. A fight where you speak to each other is easily solved and then you can cool off, but the text one prolongs the emotions to dangerous levels.

Use the highlighted rules properly and you will see the improvement in your conversation. Texting has power and you can only experience it when you do it in the right way, minding each other's emotions until you come together as a couple. The good thing is that it continues as a means of communication even long after you become one.

Conclusion

Texting is a powerful way of communicating, and with the modern gadgets, available today people are communicating fluently and constantly every passing minute. When you want t court a woman. All you need is her number and within no time, you will be exchanging lovely words that will lead to a blossoming relationship, if only you will follow the tips given in this book.

Text messaging is one of the best ways of communication where you can be as careful as you want before you pass your message, unlike when speaking where you cannot take back the words you have said, but with texting you can edit and countercheck your messages before you send them.

The guideline provided here will help you make the best of the messaging and you will be able to win the heart of the woman you are attracted to, without setting a foot out of your door. Try your luck today!

Made in the USA
Coppell, TX
28 August 2023

20911888R00046